SIFTINGS

Also by Larry Frank

Historic Pottery of the Pueblo Indians
Indian Silver Jewelry of the Southwest
The New Kingdom of the Saints
Train Stops (Short Stories)
A Land So Remote (Three Volumes)
Fragments of a Mask

SIFTINGS

Poems
by
Larry Frank

Sunstone
Press

SANTA FE

Cover drawing by Bill Acheff

Sunstone books may be purchased for educational, business, or sales
promotional use. For information please write: Special Markets Department,
Sunstone Press, P.O. Box 2321, Santa Fe, New Mexico 87504-2321.

Library of Congress Cataloging-in-Publication Data:

Frank, Larry.
    Siftings : poems / by Larry Frank.
      p. cm.
    ISBN 0-86534-445-0 (hardcover)
    I. Title.

    PS3556.R33426S57 2004
    811'.54—dc22

                2004018628

Published in

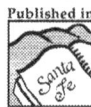

WWW.SUNSTONEPRESS.COM
SUNSTONE PRESS / POST OFFICE BOX 2321 / SANTA FE, NM 87504-2321 /USA
(505) 988-4418 / *ORDERS ONLY* (800) 243-5644 / FAX (505) 988-1025

To my unruly muse, often denied nourishment and even battered by estrangement and neglect, may we truly serve each other better with understanding and honesty.
May it be that way.

CONTENTS

PREFACE

$\mathcal{I}$t was in Europe early in the 1950s when poetry came my way as a need to gain a measure of stability and find an inner voice. The mishmash of art museums, architecture, villages, early cinema and early classical music absorbed me, but poetry was the sinew that ran through all my scramblings and tied my parts together. Anywhere, at all times, I could stop, concentrate, and do poetry.

Later in the States when I wrote and directed films for a living in Los Angeles, I carried my poetry with me as a private tune. During ten years of film work I favored certain early Russian silent film directors—Eisenstein, Pudovkin, Dovzhenko—because of their use of dynamic film editing that created a rush of searing poetic images which excited me.

From movie-making in Los Angeles to settling in Northern New Mexico in 1961 I avidly adapted to the area's distinctive landscape and Hispanic and Pueblo Indian cultures. In an adobe fortress I purchased on top of a mesa I could collect my scattered wits together and produce poetry. During these times the winters were far more severe and prolonged than now and the feat of whipping up poetry enabled me to endure those long seizures of cold, white days. Inevitably images of snow crept into my verse along with

13

an intense observation of the turnings of the naturescape around me. On the hilltop I would sift through the material I mined and carefully examine each discovery I gleaned on my fingertips, concepts large and small that in turn became small and large breaking all rules of dimension. I waited there stirring, circling, shifting.

What emerged resulted into a stretch of poetry covering a jumble of years and time-frames which melded together into a single continuum of consciousness composed of individual poems. Each poem reflects a state of being or an altered state I occupied at a particular moment, mood, encounter, experience. At one end of the spectrum a hybrid haiku that mean-spiritedly satirizes society commingles with a youthful expression of love. Each example represents a different point of view completely valid in its own right, and even when opposite views are presented they both affirm and reveal the human condition in all its complexity. Stray whims and dogged convictions equally contribute to a realm that focuses on being alive, aware, vibrant, open, charged.

Seeking images, I have followed a fruitful trail of poets and writers who have formed lasting impressions on my approach to writing—notably the grandeur of sound and visual constructs in Gerard Manley Hopkin's poems, the lyrical language of John Millington Synge's prose, the daunting spirit of Anglo Saxon bards, and the elegant and precise poetic expressions by the Japanese and Chinese poets. These were all tempered in the crucible of New Mexico.

At the end it comes down to the poetry at hand. In their diversity I hope these poems strike a responsive chord with readers and launch them on a compelling and satisfying journey.

—Larry Frank 2004

SIFTINGS

1

Winnowing the hours
I get distillations:
spotted flickers span out
and caress lingering in mid-air,
field mice scamper up when
a barrel bastion is removed,
and as I measure my pulse
there is no counterpoise
of sturdy car motors and crowds rumbling,
but the event of my life ebbing
to raccoons killing my chickens
and eating their breasts only,
or the back of their necks,
no yardstick for goals
among peopled lawns to choose from.
It matters not
whether I meandered in L.A.
or tried to be a San Diego sailor;
my life lets out to
cakes of dust banked on a buoyant river,
to leaves spinning feverishly and not dropping,
to an eagle big-as-a-dog
reluctant to leave its dead thing,
which capped a month for me,
to cottonwoods yellowing in fragments
and machete'd by early snow,
to a yellow-scruffed elk
triggering escape for a deer herd
(heightening that year);
a list of no endings and doubtful beginnings.

2

BATTLE GRIDS

On to Villalba!

Make the piston legs scar
the hills and move our
brigade and counter-brigades
to meet the Claxton town
that has no trees,
a town for mud hens on wet ground
we're miring through.
Still no sweep of martial legs
upheavals us on to Claxton,
or Villalba beyond,
though vast numbers are with us
and each second means a hamlet's hundred
        feet.
The horse stands on the tufted swell
as I remembered it years ago.

Lost we seem in the giant shake of a body
tabulating towns of people,
but when we pass well-wishers,
a dusky girl throwing fine kisses,
then I loom larger and have a power.

The next sign marker tells of Hafner-place
where we were to be at the last post;
where's Villalba on our advance?
Dry earth for once and squawking birds.
Why? When one good battle will end it,

or, if the key men as links,
stationing us along our line,
would allow with me that men,
all of them to stop this war
should surrender; to surrender is a power.

But, no, here at last is Villalba!
Now on track, we are trapped,
spurred on to launch the next attack.

On to Claxton!

3

A skein of small black birds
throws out its net
and pulls its weave together again.

4

It snowed; the mountain
marched to my front door.

5

Looking at geese
against a coverlet of
black clouds and gray
I see the end of my nose.

6

The black dog
lies on a red couch
and I watch them both.

7

Even though you and I have distinct minds
in separate places of the bed
my sheet becomes enmeshed in yours.
As I move I pull you closer,
if I remain quiet then I can stop
from ensnaring you, or even better,
force myself to sleep again.
You are invisibly caught in the strands
of my pony tail.
When I turn away from you the tangle tightens,
when I move towards you to free myself
the pull stings my eyes.
All I can do is stay still
forever drawn to you.

8

A fervid storm spends its desires
too soon
while I resume its rage
without end.

9

You begin by loving yourself
and end up wondering why.

10

Possessions are no more unimportant
than their owners.

11

I present myself with hostility,
to know a person often
leads to disappointment.

RED DRESS

You were in space, always
away in dance when my
first glance on you
bent back, an eight-year-old
balking brazen at
company's appraisal.
At home you were girded
with belts of storm crackle
and sting daring anyone
to try your worth,
and in music's trance
there was a chance for your
girth to shake off your
self-inflicted sulks
and give new birth.
I went again—that was your due;
(how much you knew you controlled!)
you went through movements
like a game, all patterned out,
but you were rich in wanting.
A visit and another triggered
exquisite lancing leaps,
and the bunched back
of a cat's attack came;
so when you flew
in fleeting swoops
you rippled in a red dress.
Between dances you pulled my nose
and (so girl-great)
flecked my hair with greens,
and I became wedged in beside

your fights and hurts.
We planned our marriage,
when you had paced through
schoolboys, like a galaxy of toys,
and under a tree-engraved
moon, kissed and laughed and spooned;
then you would touch me
beyond bliss,
and I felt
as you mastered
each chord
of my music
you would never let me go.
Your frame-silhouette has depth
and flesh; your hair's
aspect changes every day;
you no longer care for animal
names of my invention.
Two schools poured through you
and their swarm shook you
all alive, and grown boys
have mustered to you.
In your motion now there is no dance.
The red dress you wore on
daily errands you ripened
through and left limp.
Yes, your whirling sight was
but a blur then, melding
and yet shielding us from
one consuming stare.
Your step is still quick and sunlit
while my gait is flanked
by a rotund shadow.

13

While in his house
I thought of his immense
unhappiness
which made my woe turn bright.

14

I, the father, drift uncontrolled
in my son's bloodstream.

15

Watching my daughter's body swell
absorbs me less
than watching my wife's age.

16

I love the slashing sky
because it does not
account for me.

Our encounter jelled yet
perhaps I meant little to
your guileless self.
You displayed a shy note
and fleeting smile
while I emerged with
jammed words of delight—
tiny specks of adventures
so little to lean on.
For it was you who
peered down on me
resting on Cuzco's plaza steps
(I also guileless)
not thinking woman or song,
even though I arose and talked
my American opposite your Spanish.
But we did move down steps
on cobbled streets and crucified
ourselves with stark questions:
I very familied, and you half my age,
a student, poor, loverless, vulnerable.
Yes, you would manage to show me
San Blas, and yes, we together
could lock up just the
bare assemblage of an hour
before our systems made us part.

18

—or like the actor
bowing his theatrical bow
to each one watching him
in all that clattering dark,
we know our beginning
and end are equally stark.

19

When the storm passes
far away I hear
the rumble of my disgust.

20

When the mountains turn orange
I cull a few minutes
to talk to no one.

Simon, it snowed today
after you left, a big snow;
but now there was an indifference
between it and me, even with
a March snow
that too late wasted itself.
I visited our friends who glared
at the snow and seemed like me
to be outposts recording your going,
or sentinels waiting for your return;
they saw only a white puffed arrogance
that had to be mastered and sullied.
Your paintings are all over town,
at least in many hands, but they
don't hold up, (no offense)
without your being with them.
I talk to talk; I talk
now and again to the Greek hotel
man who talks about missing you,
and then I watch for movies that
you'll be seeing in London.
I listen to myself think.
Even our young waif, Felicia, today
didn't dissect the snow with her hot-
blooded, miraculous reappearances.
But this is being too concrete.
Before it snows I'll seal up the roof better.

22

My friend likes me
because he thinks I'll
be his biographer.

23

When the snow comes
my heart goes to the south
while my urine cleaves
a warm furrow in its wake.

24

Little fat, oval birds,
dark against soggy white,
eating loose seeds
like the snow better than I.

25

People complain that I
planted an olive tree
like a barbed wire at my gate
to keep them out.

THE WAR PARTY

While warring with weapons
of iron sharpness and a cunning clutch
in pursuit of those with rich stores
sunk in a lair
mossed over with coveted river green,
we ran our teeth crimson on bulbous
chokecherries and caught
yellow flicker feathers dandled to us;
took the perimeter domained in luxuriant peace
hurtled by sun,
as shadows slid and leaves curled,
and houred hints of time made us
abruptly wary of our hunting hard on course.
Our ancient cause served us as our right to strike.
Wild streamers of tangles and bloom knew us before
and welcomed us deeply under their cover;
we waited
while a fine tingle dried in our foreign tracks.

We exulted in ourselves—the unseen.

Long after our successful sacking has silted down
to thought streams quiet and clear,
when the quicksilver mind no longer daggers
afresh a relish and tribal hatred
but fragments into streaks of disgust,
after and when the deaths died darkly
 are swallowed into ground, and the booty

frayed into heaps of no matter—then
the hunting no longer shapes in a living mind
the triumph, but seeps back
into fitful memories of the defenseless village in
    lush
silence before our brutal attack strung itself
upon mating sounds snuffed out in mutilation,
leaving only the rhyming of rushing water.

27

The red willows
rear up in the snow
proud of their color.

28

Flaws enhance a landscape;
they cap humans with beauty.

29

Bruised fruit heals only
if one plants its seed.

ONE TO ONE

Wherever you are I think of you.
Like a general's map full of pins
positioning troops in war
I stab at you with concern
while you move against this background
of my almost touching you
without touching at all,
as if my fingers were little
tunnels outstretched to you.
And you, conscious that you are
recorded even in obscurity,
are augmented; we are one to
one in our logistical maneuvers,
although under different skies,
perhaps recorded in some map tucked
away in an adjutant's desk,
locked up, in between piles,
the after-fact of a lost war.

31

My thoughts are beside you
lolling with your tea bag
and rising as vapor.
The fragrance of your tea
keeps me company.

A short, tubby man,
he spoke
convictions without
the background to hold them;
he dealt to us a warm
humanity of bigotry.

Like chokecherries on a limb
just severed,
my unnourished words go on.

TENEBRES

The Penitentes know the noise for Christ is brutal,
as He lies a dead thing in metamorphosis to one
  living,
misshapen, extinct, between lives in the tomb's
  darkness,
brutal in the stifling void that ensues
after the killing,
murdered by the iron tools He knew so well...
The Penitentes cull this silence
behind walls in chaotic darkness
into a raw roar of glory,
lash out with clanging logging chains,
and with beating, pounding clubs
whirl clacking wooden toys
which become not that,
but the gnarled rhythmic groan
of the stark monster arising alive,
standing ,
on the lid of the whorled and weltered globe.

35

He left for India
which will gain that place nothing,
but stationed here
I will skim over his
wake of cruelty.

No reason
existed to battle him
since I could maim him
more with words.

The wind, dells, and I
have no need to be
described by poetry.

MY MIND

As I walk I let the day's ramblings
make my statement, but I should not;
for the day is its own construction,
forms its own mould;
yet each day is a mind's device.
Piercing through its boney room my mind
stalks the day, paws over what fascinates—
a thorough wife, sand paper hills, an insane
magpie; hurling itself into space it
crouches springing upon events;
it causes no shadow.
Once hunting the day my mind unanware
entered undimensioned woods,
seized quicksand circumstance
and traceless, was devoured.

39

The white-bellied field mice
to evade the cold
go inside my house
where I set my tiny traps.

40

The snows, the jade-hued stream,
the jay's whim simply
disengages me
from the knowledge
that men are starving
and are not free.

41

With the lightning
I live
by a jagged hatred.

The young and old go both
sweet and sour in my being.
I am accustomed to olden hope:
hero's yearnings were mine
whether of armored steeds,
Indians, or tycoons always successful,
while goodness done remained so,
unrestricted,
and a solid floor waxed by layers of peerless
virtue jutted up gleaming for the
un-born to stand solidly on.
Thank you.

Half-old I am now; caught,
moving forward I abdicate,
and I can hark back no longer.
I must readjust the part
of me the Lascaux
seers, Gregorian strains,
women of Botticelli formed;
all these things and I now
are tallies of equal value.
My fellows, our ancient wall of
achievement set in mental humus
is quite easily white-washed
in importance by the event
of a nail or an envelope,
a laser beam or a bullet.
Our poetic past dimly stands
in orderly rank to the vital

order-givers of today.
As history courses through me
I am in focus: a part of Hitler
and of others dead, part of the
H-bomb's every change in grossness,
still the last and latest specie,
still man in fact,
lavishly igniting the grave's way
with my aged legs reeling
backwards vainly seeking comfort
from old homesites, flowers, memories.

Hope shines blithely up from
the bottom of the well;
deeply imbedded
it should probably stay there.

"I was upset all the month
of January,"
she said,
and so she was,
and in February too.

Jeri despairs
that year after year
the deer eat her tulips.

The warmth of your hand
on the stone you gave me
speaks of you.

HAVEN

I was made of a tamped earth house of her,
wattled, thatched, sodded-patched my haven
love-inset and recast
with word wealth, thought grains,
whole lanes of soul cluster,
each gesture, nuance, stance, muster
felt, fought, footed by her.

My house, the sum of two, grew cold
as she grew old to it. I opened in
the bold outside din; bereft,
she found no-room a shell, and left.

In a tamped earth house of her—
wet mud, frayed sticks, dry rot,
windbreached,
O, I am a dearth of her.

48

Although the cemetery
next to my house
provides quiet neighbors,
I feel that I must
disappoint them.

49

I have killed six mice, two snakes,
and a cottontail;
I did not mind their blood
but with each day's little death
I writhe.

50

My friend in analysis
fears that when he finishes
nothing will be left
of our friendship.

51

The hours have built days
and collect a residue of years.
My Love is far from me
fingering my image
while I flutter through tints,
echoes, and falling curtains
trying to stake down what I have of her.

After we left there was
a clear frieze of us
before the tide of memory creeps back;
at any link I could have taken in our line,
and folded her form, sculpting
her kisses.

I am not old, nor is our departure,
but my walk with her is recharted,
and my thoughts are in rough grain
not filling the edges of my mental frame.

Now my pace quickens slightly,
my hair is neat over dull eyes
sleeping in their sockets.
I have lost the amber touches
she was made of love worlds ago.

TO MY LOVE

Last leaf, lost luck
my woman is a lot of fuck.

Disheveled, heavy-assed and lame
she's my woman all the same.

Graveyard cook, python will, but fearless,
my love, my dove, my coo, my Sue, is peerless.

From cactus hair to athletes' feet's
a descending description of my sweet.

Her veined complexion, rosy hue
denies the sun but craves the brew.

In my bed her dreadnaught keel
ploughs through me from head to heel.

So I declare my sweetheart's fair,
nymph, sprite, rose and grizzly bear.

ON FOREIGN ELOPEMENT

On the other side I was going,
out of my city by rail, packing
through peaked ranges on foreign elopement,
then to vessel upon
the plane of spiked seas
away from chipped and fractured faces,
I hied to the source of mystery and beloved.

On the other side I was going,
further prepared for crushing
peace plus more.
I shared with none
ingesting delights
until the land breezed out to me,
jutting spur,
fine brown glaze of dirt greened;
above, my modern bird
traced the loam of wind.

On the other side I was going,
hill goats clambered, vines nestled
in rocks, air skimmed over my back,
trees tossed tawny, and fat
butterflies bulleted over ponds
of soft clays peeping with turtles
while I watched and wafted serene,
and inside, dying, rejected the celestial scene.

My sister travels mostly,
while in between
she peers at life.

All day I work on scarred images
hoping for a poet's performance.
Badgered by time
I wait with a spidery trap
to ensnare even a stricken thought.

Under the ice encrusted stream
black water streaks visibly
in pulses
like mice scurrying for cover.

On the strength of the day he trusted;
seeing with film-flicker depth
he ran reel on.
Color tracks, odd towns
tumbled like sugar squares,
textured scent, sun glazings,
cloud tufts, baked mud walls,
storied his days taut and tested.
He told his love in Paris
that she was one of numbers
to have until their workings
reached the best of both—
when he would abacus—
add her to the score
one more, leave, and move on.
On the strength of the day he crested;
trying to stake down the minute's spine
he thrashed sprawling hours
and lives leaped in pores.
He flung the finery and force
of his life's spray
across ancient sea-backs and land-legions
that he could be like sun
and run all over.

58

When we scream at each other
often I feel content,
although I still bother
to ruffle my inner pleasures
even when I am satisfied
and can afford to
let past hungers go.

Houses built, chinked and skeletal
riddling a spinning crust
are little pegs in the earth.

BEING

He sat before me and talked
of being which only he understood.
For others he discounted their mere
state of being a life of walking
about and prosaically
breathing in and out as
the normal discord of bones
placed in friction.
He sat and as I looked he was like dead.

THE MOUNTAINS AND THE SEA

The explorer and his party
in trackless mountains,
craggy like old crone breasts
dried and long since snow-fed,
persisted in search of open waterways,
and the whole hulking stream of men
twisted through the rind of sheer
rejection until jubilant,
they jumbled onto the sea.

But the sea was just as old
and cold to them as were the shrill
crones chattering with wind in rasped tones;
for the sea swarmed with its
own ancient hags
having cursing lips and clenched fists,
gesticulating its wet roar.

With time distilled as embers
the explorer and his men
measured their lives framed by
the noise of the rising mountains
and the spume of the clashing sea.

62

Why create for such a world
he said across from me
when such a world
created us to be a blasphemy.

THE LOCKED PUZZLE

I wander the cemetery
inspecting graves endlessly decorated
and soak up beneath small parcels
the locked puzzle of human pieces
preserved in my mind—
to urgently have them stay the course of their dying
to remain as vivid as when I could
unabashedly laugh with my playmates.

64

Deeply within I have melted my feelings
into a hard shell of wax,
yet the light from the candle
I hold gleams on the varnished table.

The poets, surely, are substitutes
for the beauty of our doings, done;
for what passes actually richest,
when changed by them,
can be but a veil on the sun.
Poets once toiled their rhymes
to gaits of rising and retiring
with the seasons' menstruations—
in a clime when all was pinioned
to sheerest awe melanged by fear.
But we poets now
secrete into each other's ears,
fumble our twilly, fluted thoughts
to one or two others only;
we are substitutes, and lonely.

66

You have brought me little items,
you taught me the shapes of sand,
careful each kernel on the other
rests like pillars, the sum of one.

67

I'll love you if you'll love me,
I must have this guarantee to love.
If you'll love with no return
I'll love your love for me.

68

You are so arcane it pleases me;
my hand on you never expects,
yet stays to furrow your back
under silk. A smile
lies crinkled in my ardor.

69

When I loved you in the throes
of that fascination I
would have written love words on
chairs and cigarettes and placed
them in Egypt's tomb for
future passersby to find them.
Now they lie in knots of twisted sound.
I envy my past sojourn
into the citadel of love.

RELATED TO GERALD MANLEY HOPKINS

In England England's good God, yours,
turns on leaf, twig, branch, elm,
and converts safe rain showers
into a twist of water that shears
free—on a glistening deer. Here,
all in scale to walks with tender eye
coifed around landscape fallen ordered
a green God stirs in symmetry, though
odd at times, but odd in unity.
The
       ancient
           monster
                Grendel has little roam
precisioned in downs and clipped hedges,
can hardly mar a green state in God's grace,
a wimpled dimpled heaven haven home.
Yet Grendel scratched us deadly before the green
God won his clime in our hearts;
his fiery roar in scale to Nuremberg
and brown Storm Troopers roaring,
and fires roaring in symmetry
to burning books, to burning England.

An incendiary dragon that first slithered
in our mind can no longer be contained;
the green God now must share his reign.

THE MOPPET

My sprout, my son,
must you learn about
the evil one;
must around your two years'
trunk a growth-ring form
made of hell's ditch and out
of blackness comes the witch;
should you know the giant's thunder
rending innocence asunder;
can you be saved from brutes, my son,
the clown's grief and derision,
or must you be forever made a
manacled moppet in our prison.

72

My friends scale down
to a stack of gestures:
the rooms are the same,
food's not worthwhile to bother with,
their thoughts are tattered originals,
and guests can be compensated for;
only humor endures.

73

PLAZA DE SERVILLETTA, NEW MEXICO

the town's   roads are snowed upon
river   too often,
bulges   children long out of school
darkening   linger in
a greenness   houses frayed with people
trenchant   in ones or one more
through orchards   who think alone,
fielded   ideas fall singly
among spread   to the floor.
livestock.   Broken.

78

The earth shifts, impacts upon itself,
sifts;
mountains wear away by fractions,
tear;
the sea lies fallow in itself,
dries;
the sun flumes upon its core,
consumes;
the heart fickles freely,
apart.

75

I phase away, turned off.
The monkeys prevail.
There are no advances on any
course, we know that.
All points menace, explode,
undo the past I'm moored to,
the present I'm wedged in.
Knee-deep in our flabby hearts
handsprings come hard now.
Which way to life closing down?
All ways are ways to no way.
It's still wrong to waste time
but all time is a waste.
And only today are doctors ignoble pests.
Even death is dull, a dose of banality.
I had a girl who is like the other girl.
Why girl? My house allows me a tomb.
I still get up and kill flies.

The old man showed me the photos.
"The photos tell the story," he said.
One showed him sixteen, the other
his seventy-four years.
"What happened?" he puzzled.
If he meant death he should have said it;
if gradually his circuitry misfired,
his hamstrings nibbled on by time
he should have said death
so I could with no hesitation
have lined up against it.

77

Uninvolved,
I am so free
that it scares me,
free not to choose
what I wanted
when I was less free,
free to choose
nothing at all.

78

We search seas, hurt:
bolted from the Wound-Spurter
we carry embedded iron
shafts with rippling ropes
dragging through the pillowed
seas we dearly seek.
When the slack comes taut
the span of man is caught.

79

You are worried, tiny flurried
tracks trace around your married eyes
that dim perceptibly.
We could invent love in 1972.
We have dabbled deep in creations,
can transmute all substances but ourselves.
My hand on your breast is my life's duration
which speeds the world revolutions faster.
Our minds dovetail as one.   .
I cannot unlove you, yet
you are worried; I cannot
push the worrying aside.
Your terrain with children
cannot be landscaped away.
Our gait jars out of sync,
our hair sheds differently,
sadly our best words bump.
Back we go where we came from,
where we have been, to the
dark garage of our childhood.

The sun hums for me
and I for it
and we both know
our tuning is true.
The sun would still hum
if I did not
ripple in its spectrum,
but yes the sun hums for me
and I for it
and that we both know.

THE WALK OF AEONS

He on the road
walked with toes splayed
as feet webbed, stiff and cold,
scattering rocks
and being knifed by those
anchored in the ancient ground.
The Christ man stumbled on jagged shard,
splintering nails,
pumping each leg up the hard hill
filled with spiny stone age plants
which barely broke His ankle skin.
He trampled on course
 where the great armored beasts long before Him
lumbered, groping for their extinction.

82

It amounts to the mountain;
I cannot step around it
since it positions my mind.
Only I climb my mental
ridges and slip often.
To fall from the top is expected.

She thought not;
not was very good to think about
and better than some
unstable idea to harbor,
so she chose not to think at all.

To read is an error,
to write is worse
if you presume beyond
the wonder to touch.

THE FISH

"I feel my blood run through its
tangled bed,"
my friend's poem said in its last line
about a fish seen and felt for,
a bloodless fish willed into hot being
by my friend carving out its zone
in the darting shadows of his mind
and flopping it onto a pure stream-bed
nestled weightless under the comforter of waters.

He, big-boned and with his boots,
enormous pant bottoms and black barb-wire hair
went into the pores of the fish and lived there
caught in halves of light and dark,
waiting for the arbitrary waters to recede
and catch its lungs quivering death on wet sand.

Perhaps, it's kinder if he remains so obscured—
that his bulk lurks hidden in shapes
and sizes unknown
with the night passing freely through his head
and the stars above him seen filtered
through ceilings of water,
absent from corridors of intelligence,
allowed to die silently, easily, like his fish,
                              undefiled.

Green turquoise in a dry, yellow land;
Green and blue lost in a giant's space;
Green fertility woven into myth;
Green, soft stone the reincarnation of a dead bloom;
Green reflecting the sky's underwater flow;
Green-blue stone on a somber, dark-earthed Navajo,
Green thoughts weathered on the land of his face;
Green tipped and blue bodied run the rare storm drops;
Green turquoise in a dry, yellow land.

WORDS

I resent words written, mine
socked down on paper ending as words,
stop-seamed, trapped as trout.
I resent your reading them as
breakfast food, fixed preparations,
when they don't mean that or this or what
you think I thought but squirm off-angle.
I detest spiked eyes in mental prisons
that claim my words and change their
composition into bed ticking.
I like my words to coalesce into themselves,
untouched and not philandered, still
limitless in intent as freshets of finches,
still mine not yours I keep them.
Afraid to demonstrate, suspicious that
my work is stale or you are worse
I tighten my sphincters
to outwait each day that comes like a ton.

When I pass his house
I know we would be friends,
but because he has a woman
I stay away bummed.

Wafted on flowing waters
my own course ebbs:
burrs, reeds, skein, twigs,
straw wads latch
slightly matted, catch,
then shredded apart by
the uncaught hook of volition—
my life so unmade, I am afraid.

Sadly the lingering snow
finally left me,
unfortunately
my woman has not.

SILENCES

On a long trip with you
we talked in the silent muted stretches,
glided on inaudible runners of feelings
warily shadowed by few words, our failures.
The words we dulled by
casting them as sprung rabbits,
then unleashed our watch
dogs to shred them;
we created these small and wanton deaths.
Conscious we were that
voiceless to each other we coped
with our haplessness as
long-standing walls
rasped by sullen winds
over their undecipherable runes.

92

The badger tunnels through loam to light.
He knows not the sinuous caverns within his snout
nor the storied corridors of his skull
where the black scent of soil resides
in the casket of bone,
bone on the burrows of earth,
sun through the widening clawed-out dirt
sending in fractured light
from the outside that
the animal instinctively craves.

93

I am incrementally happier
when I see a frog,
pods of rain, my
window measled by drops,
twilit apples, drab
coats of shadows—
harvests freely gleaned.

94

On the white mountain a cloud of icy squalls
spreads as a congestion of one thousand beasts
blowing their vapors and battering
across the drifts on the peaks.

Evenly, historically, new snow
touches on dots, jags, dangles on dirt and leaf;
none but soft snow sought so pointedly,
unsparingly tendril, line, bloom, and
managed that tenderly to stroke my feelings.

BEYOND SPACES

Here in my fastness of heart,
in my landlocked body,
here in this land I invented
where I tarry so long,
where the mountains support me,
I hear your cry of spent ashes
almost perversely,
like the fall of powder landing
nowhere except around my ground.
I hear you, your pain, your voice,
and I must, must break a track
through your powder, my snow,
and blunt the wind with my desire
to just graze you, and in passing,
let the girth of the writhing mountains
encircle you. Let it be like that.

When you go far away
the bed sheets
thrash into knots.

Black dots of insects are
swallowed by larger insects
then devoured by fish
gulped by larger fish
falling prey to otter
killed by panther
that's felled by man
who's eaten by . . . God.

We are battered by those marching on to Walsenburg
to war,
coated with their sweat and tongues spewing words
of war
who are marching on to Walsenburg, to Walsenburg
to war—
against us who cannot fight them or save them
but can desist from all operations in support
of war
and dispose of any cog or prop if
we can find anything
of ours
that helps hold their militarized pace
in place.
We simply will remove a flag or creed
or god we've had
or whatever's been part of a history
of marching on to war.

100

You died on me,
so naturally it hurt because
of the ease you meted out to yourself.
Your organs quit, mine did not
and still gasp, rattle and puke unseen by you.
With a scorpion at your throat
for the last months you weren't much,
just blurs of noise and shabby movement.
Yet each jetted impulse
of your bony shamble corrected me,
gave my flatness dimension.
Yes, you still did chores,
and we spoke like points of reference,
yet we spoke!
But you're incorruptibly dead now
and your spirit is flat dead.
The chores get done, the children
are happier, you don't growl,
but don't care either;
you'll still growl wherever you are;
my life's keener and afresh,
I still have a young body.
I'd be more satisfied though
if I could know what you're thinking
and if you could know how we are.
My anger rises for you dying on me.

Do not say you cannot
love so young and fresh
as once you did your others
besieging their pathways
with deep deliverance of joy.
I want your exact calibration of
each past sensation
transplanted on my shore.
And—I want I want more.

Be not my mother, glide not
a burr through my terrain
scarring its land a pock and fumarole.
We can be rock to rock in warm current and no more.
Must you die on me into me.
If your days are striated by
an uneven sun, each a wastrel puppy
weaned dead, then close up, off.
For you shall not shine in me rankling forth;
I daily drain the dross from myself of you.

CHRISTMAS EVE DANCE, SAN FELIPE PUEBLO

In a timber-rafted, adobe church
I heard a priest sermonize
that when Christ came to man
he did so in meekness,
and not by crushing force.
The priest left
and animal-headdressed men
came to dance.
Buffalo and deer figures sweated
the air with their bestiality,
a brazen uncontested
legacy which moved like a
ferocious fable.
Then replacing them, shrilling,
pecking
     winged
          eagle
               dancers
wedged into the drooping nave,
vaulted up to the altar,
and flapping, embraced it—
so abandoned by the priest.

TIDES

We sit with glazed glances
like ship prows docked
and stirring listlessly
while facing uncertain waters,
denying any miscreant
words issuing between us
that would agitate our tide.
We like to cruise and skirmish
without crashing our feelings,
but are caught in little
reeling battles on vague war grids.

My boy runs ramrod against me,
still contained within my means.
Sheared to raw male
he'll not be as one
terraced within my shade,
no youth hung to his father's frame
but will surge through my shanty
as Sprung-man.
He wants rapaciously
breathings of every creature,
the tuber root free of ice.
He must break into me,
give to me, be, and beyond me.

PRISM

Afraid, my daughter calls me in the night;
I leave my wife's side to comfort her.
Between the one and another
I can't tell you...
The mountain snow hermetically
seals me,
its white angular prism baits
and hones my ingrown eye.
Between its core and mine
I can't tell you...
One day through the mountains I touched my wife
and through her the mountains.
Between each magnitude I live
I can't tell you...
I am afraid of the wilderness
of our bondage.

Wild strength steers the gull reeling
toward sea-packed life, a drab
harlequin fitted to scavenge
who skitters both mean and timid
on the same hop
while warily it insures that
its beak not be smashed sideways
and its scuffled feathers cover
the commandments of its racing
heart's breast. The bird careens
over eerie, errant earth, infusing
its bumptious pride into cracks and groans
of a spinning realm that gave it birth.

Time came upon me,
fell in a great hurry;
a flurry of wandering
time strode upon me
unleashing racing years
to file their course on my face;
a blunt wedge of time
hurled at me, felling
trees in my grove of years
leaving one stand untouched,
staring back.

Love, love me less;
leave a pore, save a mole,
keep a dash from my control.
Let it be uncharted
of stray folds blown
swirled like a Romanesque
world, or the coastline of the
lower lip condensed to kiss.
Let me taste, not swallow;
if you withhold, I'll follow.

www.ingramcontent.com/pod-product-compliance
Lightning Source LLC
Chambersburg PA
CBHW020516100426
42813CB00030B/3268/J